Uncle Henry's New Orleans

by Vernon Landry
illustrated by Dani Jones

Harcourt
SCHOOL PUBLISHERS

Printed in China

ISBN 10: 0-15-350495-1
ISBN 13: 978-0-15-350495-2

Ordering Options
ISBN 10: 0-15-350333-5 (Grade 3 Below-Level Collection)
ISBN 13: 978-0-15-350333-7 (Grade 3 Below-Level Collection)
ISBN 10: 0-15-357482-8
ISBN 13: 978-0-15-357482-5

11 12 13 14 15 0940 12 11 10

I was ten years old the first time I walked through the French Quarter of New Orleans. Dad and I were visiting Uncle Henry, who lived there.

Uncle Henry pointed out beautiful balconies. Plants in baskets hung on the railings, which were all made of iron.

"That's mine," he remarked.

"You live there?" I asked.

"No. I fixed the ironwork. I am a blacksmith," Uncle Henry explained.

"A hundred years ago, people used horses to get around. Horses wore iron shoes to protect their hooves. Blacksmiths made those horseshoes. Then cars replaced horses. Just a few people work as blacksmiths now, and I'm one of them.

"I repair many iron balconies in the French Quarter, and I even make a few horseshoes," he laughed.

4

"I wish I could do what you do," I said.

"Do you like it here in New Orleans, Josh?" Dad asked me.

"Yes!" I answered. "This place is great! The old buildings are really cool."

"I'm glad," answered Dad, "because we have a surprise for you. We are moving to New Orleans!"

My day was ruined. How could we move? I would have to change schools, and I would not see my friends anymore.

"Why should I be yanked away from home?" I asked. "Detroit is everything I know."

"Mom and I both got good jobs here in New Orleans," said Dad.

"Couldn't I stay in Detroit?" I asked. "Couldn't I stay with Stefan? His mom says I'm like one of the family."

"You can write to Stefan," Dad said. "I know you will make new friends."

"When are we moving?" I asked.

"In two weeks," Dad replied.

Those two weeks flew by just as
shooting stars streak across the sky.
Movers helped us pack. Stefan came over
to my house, and I went to his house. We
tried to act normal, but we were both sad.

On moving day, the van drove away. My parents and I took a cab to the airport. The cab crept through traffic. We flew to New Orleans, and Uncle Henry met us.

New Orleans seemed less glorious now. I sat quietly in the back seat of the car. Uncle Henry drove to a garage and stopped. Was this our new home?

"Come, Josh," said my uncle. I walked
with him to the building. He opened the
door and turned on the light.

This was Uncle Henry's workshop!
I looked around. I saw an anvil, tools,
a huge oven, and beautiful ironwork.

"I have nine big repair jobs over in the French Quarter," said Uncle Henry. "School starts in three weeks. Could you help me until then? Think about it."

I didn't have to think about it. I just said "yes."

That was thirty years ago. Now I live in Detroit again. I work as a lawyer, but I also have a hobby. I go to my workshop in the garage. I use tools and an anvil to make decorations with iron. Uncle Henry's craft is more than a memory for me. It is alive and well.

Think Critically

1. Why is Josh's family moving?

2. Do you think this story could be true? Explain.

3. Why do you think Uncle Henry asked Josh to help him in his workshop?

4. What is a lesson that this story teaches?

5. Which event do you think is most important in this story? Explain.

 Art

Draw and Create A horseshoe is U-shaped. Use your imagination to draw some special horseshoes! Then think of other animals and draw some "shoes" for them, too!

School-Home Connection This story is set thirty years ago. Ask a family member to point out things in your neighborhood or in your house that are around thirty years old.